ROBERT BURNS' SCOTLAND

by Rev. J. A. Carruth M.A.

Jarrold Colour Publications Norwich

Origins and Early Years

In 1787 when Robert Burns was 28 years old he wrote to a friend some details of his life up to then. This gives us in the poet's own words a very good survey of his father, himself, and family circumstances.

'I have not the most distant pretense to what is called a Gentleman. When in Edinburgh last winter, I got acquainted at the Herald's Office. Looking through the granary of honours, I there found almost every name in the kingdom; but for me—

My ancient but ignoble blood,
Has crept thro' scoundrels since the flood.'

Burns's forefathers rented land of the Keiths of the Earl Marischal family. His grandfather farmed some of their land near Stonehaven in Kincardineshire and may have been with the tenth Earl Marischal who fought in the 1715 Jacobite Rising. The poet's own father, William Burness or Burnes (1721–84), may have been implicated in the 1745 Jacobite Rising, when Bonnie Prince Charlie and his brave Highlanders fought their way as far as Derby only 110 miles from London.

Burns himself mentions how his ancestors had fought for the Stuarts, a name once respected as he says.

My fathers that name have revered on a throne:
My fathers have died to right it;
Those fathers would spurn their degenerate son,
That name should he scoffingly slight it.

In 1786 the poet wrote an 'Address to Edinburgh'. He alludes to the fact that reinforcements from Edinburgh had joined the army of Bonnie Prince Charlie in the 1745 Jacobite Rising:

Haply my sires have left their shed,
And fac'd grim danger's loudest roar,
Bold following where your fathers led.

In 1794 Burns wrote two famous songs, 'Charlie, he's my darling' and 'It was a' for our rightful King' which show his sympathy with the Jacobite cause. Sir Walter Scott was fond of these songs and frequently sang them.

About 1750 Burns's father, William Burness (or Burnes), came to Ayrshire and leased seven acres in Alloway, near Ayr. He built a two-roomed clay cottage which is still standing. This cottage has been visited by very many, for it is the birthplace of Robert, his genius son. In December, 1757, William married Agnes Brown, a farmer's daughter from Carrick, that part of Ayrshire south of the river Doon. She was a cheerful and good wife and used to sing to her children the old Scots ballads. There were seven children to the marriage, four boys and three girls. Robert the poet, the eldest, was born at Alloway on 25th January, 1759. In 1785, when 26, Burns wrote of his birth:

Our monarch's hindmost year but ane [one]
Was five-and-twenty days begun,
'Twas then a blast o' Janwar' win'
Blew hansel (as a first gift) in on Robin.

Regarding the name 'Burness' – this two-syllable name was the family name. In 1786 Robert and his brother Gilbert, 20 months his junior, agreed to contract it into 'Burns', which was the usual form in Ayrshire where they were born and educated.

Burns's father was a hard-working, God-fearing man and he took great trouble to give his family all the education he could. Burns also owed much as he says 'to an old maid of my mother's [an old lady maintained in the family house] who had, I suppose, the largest collection in the country of tales and songs concerning devils, ghosts, fairies, witches, warlocks, spunkies, kelpies, enchanted towers, giants, dragons, etc. This cultivated the latent seeds of Poesy.' Thus the young boy was laying up material all unconsciously for 'Tam O' Shanter', 'Address to the Deil (Devil)' and other poems.

Education

When 6, Robert went for a few months to a school at Alloway. The teacher left soon after. So Burns's father along with some neighbours engaged a Mr J. Murdoch as a teacher, boarding him in their houses by turns and paying him a salary. Of this the boy wrote later:

'I was a good deal noted for a retentive memory and a stubborn sturdy "something" in my disposition. I made an excellent English scholar and by ten or eleven I was absolutely a critic in substantives, verbs and particles.'

When Mr Murdoch left, the poet's father taught them arithmetic and other subjects, and procured them books from Ayr.

Sometimes Mr Murdoch visited them and read to them. When about 15 Robert spent three weeks with him in Ayr where he carefully revised his English grammar and learned some French and Latin. He was also reading Shakespeare, Pope's 'Homer', the works of the Scots poet Alan Ramsay, and the Bible. It is quite remarkable how Robert, with the little formal education he had, was able to write such good English, for this was really a foreign language to him. As we see in most of his poems he was best able to express himself in his native Scots dialect full of very expressive words and phrases, such as 'sonsie' – having sweet, engaging looks, 'billie' – companion, 'brawly' – perfectly, 'blether' – talking idly or foolishly, 'bonnie' – lovely or handsome,

Near the fishing port of Stonehaven in what used to be Kincardineshire, Robert Burns's grandfather farmed land leased from the famous family of Keith of Marischal.

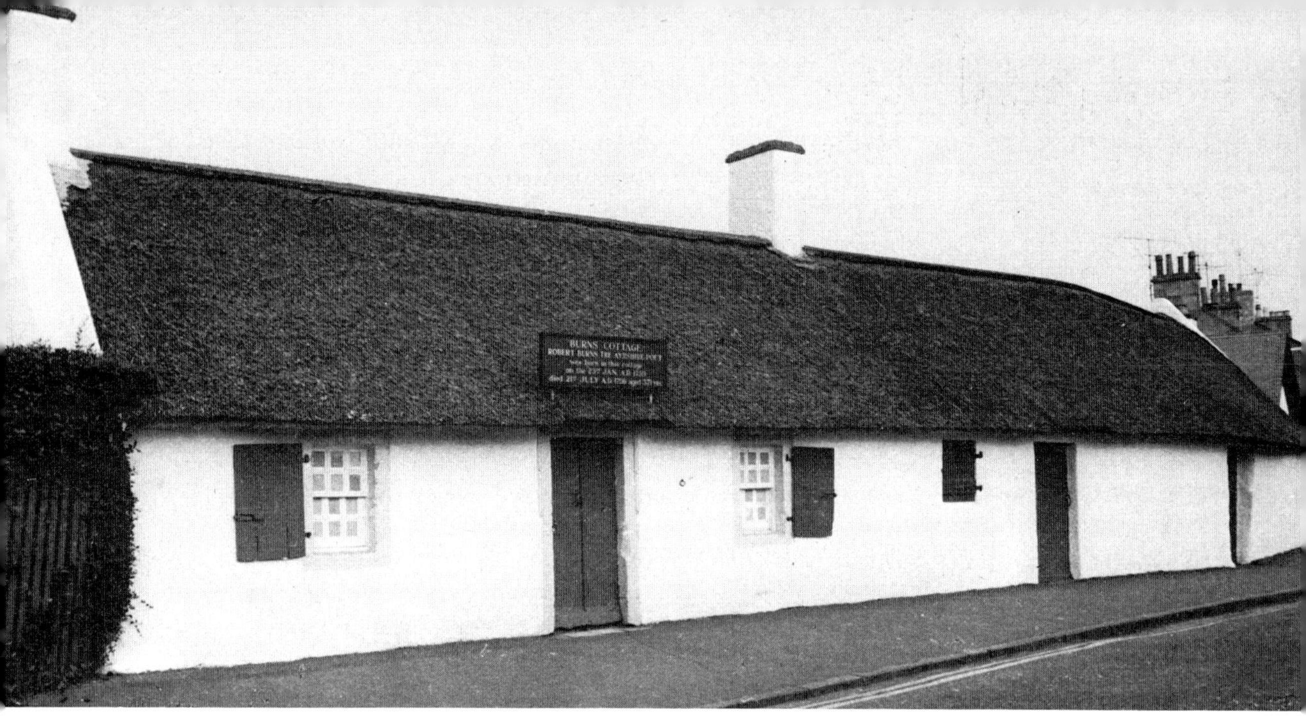
BURNS COTTAGE
ROBERT BURNS THE AYRSHIRE POET

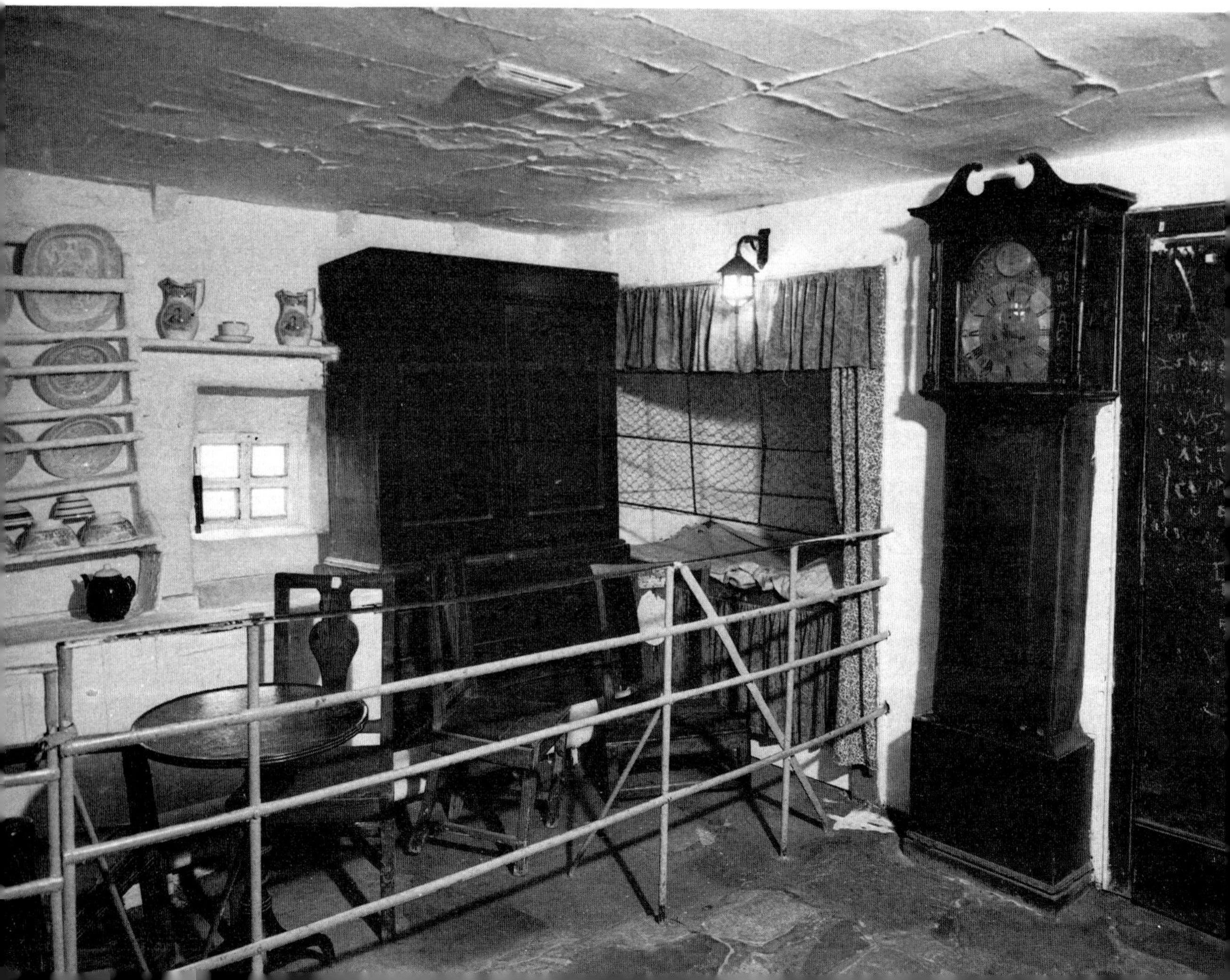

'tapsalteerie' – topsy-turvy, 'lug' – ear and many others.

The father did not neglect his family's religious upbringing. His immortal memory is depicted for all time by his poet son in 'The Cotter's Saturday Night' where he movingly describes how the 'saint, the father and the husband prays, kneeling down to Heaven's eternal King'. That saint, father and husband is the poet's own father.

The cottage in Alloway where Robert Burns was born and spent the first seven years of his life.

This picture of the kitchen shows the bed in which Robert was born.

Below: *The Byre adjoining the living quarters.*

This undying picture of Christian family prayer was written throughout in English, whereas most of Burns's best poems and songs are in the lowland Scots language.

His father also composed, probably with some help, 'A Manual of Religious Belief' which can still be read with profit. Perhaps his piety was somewhat strict, but then so was the piety of many Christians, Catholic and Protestant, at that time. Perhaps too our permissive society could learn something in this respect. Due mainly to the teaching and example he received from his father, Robert remained a believing and practising Christian in spite of difficulties caused by his temperament, temptations and bad example.

Left: *The grave of William Burns. The inscription reads: 'Sacred to the memory of William Burns of Lochlie who died on the 13th February 1784 in the 63rd year of his age. And of Agnes Brown his spouse who died on the 15th January 1820 in the 88th year of her age.' She was interred in Bolton Churchyard, East Lothian.*

Below: *The River Doon and Burns Monument seen from the 'Auld Brig o' Doon'.*

Burns and Morality

It is true that Burns had his moral lapses, but he fought against them. He fell and he rose again. One recalls his touching poem, 'Welcome to his love-begotten daughter', written in 1784 when he was 25:

> *Lord grant that thou may inherit*
> *Thy mother's person, grace and merit,*
> *And thy poor worthless daddy's spirit,*
> *Without his failings.*

'I'll never rue my trouble wi' thee, but be a loving father to thee.' One is reminded how St Augustine called his natural son 'God-given'. Both men lapsed, both repented, both expressed their repentance in immortal literature.

One of Burns's best friends was the Catholic Bishop, John Geddes, for whom the poet had a high regard. In 1787 Burns wrote of him: 'The first (best) Cleric character I ever saw was a Roman Catholic', though later Burns was to have much help and sympathy from Protestant clergymen also. The poet wrote a truly remarkable letter to the Bishop in 1789: 'I have now not only the retired leisure but the hearty inclination to attend to those great and important questions – what am I? where am I? and for what am I destined?'

Burns then went on to tell the Bishop how his habitual follies could not be justified by any sophistry. In addition he was responsible for the happiness or misery of his dear wife and he could not trifle with such a desposit.

With reference to this letter the Bishop commented: 'If any man, after perusing this letter, will still say that Burns was a scoffer

Robert Burns turning up a mouse in her nest while ploughing: engraving by John le Conte.

at Revelation, that man need not be
reasoned with, as his own mind must be
hopelessly beyond the reach of argument.'

While on the subject of Burns's moral
lapses, a word may be said about drink.
Burns wrote in praise of ale and whisky.
Many writers in many literatures have
written in praise of drink. The Bible itself
is quite eloquent on the subject. In fact, it
seems to sum it all up when it says: 'Wine
was made to make men merry and not to
make them drunk.'

Burns is of the same opinion. Here is a
passage from his 'Scotch Drink' written in
1785 when he was 26:

When heavy-dragged with pain an' grieving
　　But oiled by thee,
The wheels o' life go down-hill, scrievin,
　　(gliding swiftly)
　　Wi rattlin glee.
When neibors anger at a plea (lawsuit)
An' just as wud (mad) as wud can be,
How easy can the barley-brie (whisky)
　　Cement the quarrel.

And the poet prefaces his poem with a
quotation from the Proverbs of Solomon in
praise of drink.

The testimony of 'Bonnie Jean', Burns
wife, is specially noteworthy in this
connexion. S. McKenzie has recorded how
she told him with tears in her eyes that in
all her knowledge of her husband either
before marriage or after she never once saw
him intoxicated. Never once did she know
him having to be seen home or in the least
difficulty when he did arrive home.

This enables us to form a better idea of
Burns's moral failings. If failings they were,
they were failings of frailty. To be unkind
or unjust, to calumniate or slander others
– these are more than the failings of frailty.
Of these Burns was rarely guilty, if at all.

The poet was indeed grateful to those
who helped him. He owed much, as we saw,
to his father's religious teaching and good
example. His son acknowledged this in the
touching epitaph he wrote for his father's

tombstone in Alloway Churchyard when
the latter died worn out with toil and
hardship in 1784 when his son was aged 25:

THIS STONE WAS ERECTED TO THE
MEMORY OF WILLIAM BURNESS,
WHO DIED FEBY. 13, 1784
AND WAS BURIED HERE.

O ye whose cheek the tear of pity stains,
　Draw near with pious reverence and attend!
Here lie the loving Husband's dear remains,
　The tender Father, and the gen'rous Friend;
The pitying heart that felt for human woe;
　The dauntless heart that feared no human
　　pride;
The friend of man, to vice alone a foe;
　For e'en his failings leaned to virtue's side.

Fortunate father to live for ever in his famous
son's immortal tribute!

The Young Poet
1773–1784

Burns and his brothers and sisters had helped
their father with the family farm, and the
poet mentions how he 'was a dexterous
ploughman' for his years. He had also
developed into a sturdy young man, and had
made the most of all the education he had
been able to get. When he was 14, the girl
who was helping him in the harvest sang
a song she said was composed by a small
country laird's son. 'I saw no reason why I
might not rhyme as well as he', Burns
wrote, and thus he composed his first poem
'Handsome Nell'. And from then till his
death about twenty-three years later those
poems and songs came tumbling out, giving
delight and joy to the poet himself, his
countrymen and all the world. It was as his
father had once predicted: 'Rab will one
day become famous.'

Burns had learned to plough and reap on
his father's farms. The first was at Mount
Oliphant, 4 miles from Ayr, where he lived

Wellington Square, Ayr.

The Bachelors' Club founded in 1780 at Tarbolton by Robert Burns, his younger brother Gilbert, and five other young men.

The Portrait of Robert Burns by Alexander Nasmyth. Scottish National Portrait Gallery.

from 1766 to 1777, i.e. from his 7th to 18th
year. In 1777 the family moved to the farm
of Lochlea in the parish of Tarbolton,
7 miles from Ayr, where they remained till
1784, i.e. from the poet's 18th to 25th year.
In 1782 he went for a short time to Irvine to
learn flax-dressing. The premises there
took fire, and Burns humorously says of this:
'Our shop was burned to ashes and left me,
like a true poet, not worth a sixpence.'

> *O why the deuce should I repine*
> > *And be an ill foreboder?*
> *I'm twenty-three and five feet nine,*
> > *I'll go and be a sodger (soldier).*

In 1780 when Burns was 21, he himself,
his brother Gilbert and five other young
men established at Tarbolton the 'Batchelors'
Club'. Meetings were held monthly and
questions debated. No member was to spend
more than threepence. He continued
writing poetry and during this time
composed 'The Tarbolton Lasses', a para-
phrase of Psalm 1, and 'A Prayer in the
prospect of Death'. In this poem the
essentially Christian belief that God is love
and that He delights in showing mercy is
very well expressed:

> *Where with intention I have erred,*
> > *No other plea I have.*
> *But Thou art good: Goodness still*
> > *Delighteth to forgive.*

In 1786 he paraphrased this in his 'Address
to the Unco Guid' (Very Good) as:

> *Then gently scan your brother man*
> > *Still gentler sister woman.*
> *Tho' they may gang (go) a kennin wrang*
> > *(a little wrong),*
> > *To step aside is human.*

Coming from a young man of 27 with
little formal education this poem with its
balanced blending of kindness, wit and
wisdom has few equals in any language.
Burns's humour is spontaneous, true to life
and always fresh. I think of his delicious
fable 'The Twa Dugs' (The Two Dogs)
written in the same year, 1786, as the
previous poem. This humorous fable can
rank with the best of Aesop and La Fontaine.
When the dogs had finished dissecting the
foibles of men

> *Up they got an' shook their lugs (ears)*
> *Rejoiced they were na (not) men but dugs.*

How felicitous is his use of the old Scots
word for 'ears', and what deep humour in
the finality of the end line. The last word
has been said. At least so the dogs think, in
common with many men on many topics.
The reader of Burns will come across many
other examples of his delicious and
penetrating humour.

Burns's sense of humour was not confined
to the written word. He was witty in speech
as well. Just after his death in 1796 a lady
who knew him well, wrote:

'None ever outshone Burns in the charms
of fascinating conversation. His wit would
lead him into raillery uniformly acute, but
often unaccompanied with the least desire
to wound.' This same person seems to me
to sum up that characteristic which all
really great men have possessed when she
adds: 'Burns was candid and manly in the
avowal of his errors, and his avowal was a
reparation.' In our best moments we know
we want to do as Burns did.

'Bonnie Jean' and Highland Mary, 1784–1786

After his father's death in February 1784,
Robert with others of the family leased
Mossgiel Farm near Mauchline in Ayrshire.
In April 1784, Burns now 25 first got to
know his future wife, 'Bonnie Jean' – Jean
Armour, though they were not able to marry
officially till 1788. In 1786 Burns seemed to
have misjudged her while she was under

heavy pressure from her father to have nothing to do with Burns.

Misfortunes now came thick and fast on the poet. The farm at Mossgiel was a failure. Jean had left him. There seemed no hope left. So he resolved to emigrate to Jamaica and to publish his poems to raise his passage money. In June 1786 he wrote to his Freemason Brethern of the Tarbolton Lodge his poem 'The Farewell'. Burns had become a Freemason about two years previously and he was to remain an enthusiastic member till he died in 1796. In the masonic rites and ceremonies he found an outlet for that liking for ritual and pageantry so dear to him.

Perhaps in consequence of Jean's apparent jilting of him, the poet became deeply attached to Mary Campbell, the 'Highland Mary' of the poem of that name. Here is one stanza of the touching poem he composed about her, his 'Highland Lassie':

The tomb of 'Highland Mary' (Mary Campbell) who died at Greenock in October 1786.

But fickle fortune frowns on me,
And I maun (must) cross the raging sea;
But while my crimson currents flow,
I'll love my Highland Lassie, O.

He proposed marriage, she accepted and they had a touching and deeply moving farewell before she left for Argyll to see her parents about the marriage. This farewell was on Sunday, May 14th, 1786, when they met on the banks of the river Ayr. They vowed eternal fidelity and sealed their vow by exchanging Bibles. The Bible the poet gave her is now preserved in Burns's birthplace at Alloway. Burns was moved to the depths of his being by this episode. He never saw his 'Highland Lassie' again, for Mary died in October 1786, and was buried in Greenock. This news, of course, again affected Burns very deeply and for years after. In 1789 he wrote the sad and moving poem in her honour: 'To Mary in Heaven.'

Eternity can not efface
Those records dear of transports past,
Thy image at our last embrace,
Ah! little thought we 'twas our last!
That sacred hour can I forget,
Can I forget the hallow'd grove,
Where, by the winding Ayr, we met,
To live one day of parting love!

Rise to fame, Edinburgh, 1786

At Kilmarnock in Ayrshire Burns published his poems in August 1786. Their success was instantaneous. Burns, like Byron, awoke one morning and found himself famous. Such original poetry, so natural and so expressive, so humorous and so tender, had not appeared since Shakespeare. The twenty-seven-year-old countryman had given the world such immortal masterpieces as 'The Cotter's Saturday Night', 'To a

The Castle, Scott Monument and Princes Street, Edinburgh.

Mouse', 'Holy Willie's Prayer', 'Scotch Drink', 'To a Mountain Daisy', 'Rantin', 'Rovin' Robin' and 'Hallowe'en'.

Burns was so encouraged by the kind and warm reception given to his poems that he resolved to go to Edinburgh, an excellent centre for such a man as he now was. Here he was made very welcome and he was introduced to the nobility, gentry and other eminent people. All were favourably impressed by his modesty regarding his great achievement, his brilliant conversational powers and his self-possessed bearing and behaviour. In April 1787 a second edition of his poems appeared in Edinburgh; 3,000 copies were printed – a very large number for those times. Among those who subscribed for this edition were several noblemen, one hundred members of the Caledonian Hunt and his dear Catholic friend, Bishop Geddes, who procured subscriptions from the Scottish Catholic Colleges abroad and also from the Scottish Benedictine Abbey in Regensburg, Germany, now at Fort Augustus, Highland Region, where one of its members is now writing these lines on beloved Rabbie, as the Scots affectionately call him.

In this Edinburgh edition there were some new poems, such as 'The Brigs (Bridges) of Ayr', his touching 'Address to Edinburgh' and his humorous 'Address to a Haggis'. The Kilmarnock and Edinburgh editions of his poetry made Burns very dear to his fellow-Scots, for these poems and others which followed gave literary expression to the feelings as well as to the tastes of the Scots at a time when distinctly Scottish characteristics were in danger of being submerged especially by those of England.

The picture by Hardie of the meeting of Burns and Scott at Sciennes House, Edinburgh. Radio Times Hulton Picture Library.

The kind poet. Sir Walter Scott

Burns made about £400 from the publication of the Edinburgh edition of his poems. He immediately sent about £200 to help his brother, Gilbert, who was farming at Mossgiel, Ayrshire, where their mother was also living. She survived till 1820 and thus had the great satisfaction of enjoying the growing fame of her poet son, for whom her husband and herself had worked and toiled so hard. One feels sorry that the poet's father who died, as we saw, in 1784, did

not share in this satisfaction, for he, perhaps more than anyone, was responsible for developing the latent goodness and genius of his gifted son.

And one of the most engaging traits of this son was his goodness and kindness. Burns loved to give presents. The large sum for those days he sent to his brother, Gilbert, has already been mentioned. In 1787 he had a monument erected at considerable trouble and at his own expense to the Scottish poet Robert Fergusson (1750–74). Later he was to send a barrel of brandy to Mrs Dunlop of Dunlop, a very dear friend and correspondent, the recipient of at least 42 letters from the poet. The fact that he made time in his short life of 37 years to write so many letters – at least 538 are extant – is likewise another proof of his kindness to and interest in others. The famous 'Clarinda' correspondence with Mrs M'Lehose helped both of them through a trying time.

About this time, 1786–7, Sir Walter Scott, then around 15 had his famous meeting with his revered countryman. Here is Scott's account of the meeting:

'Burns's person was strong and robust. He had a sort of dignified plainness and simplicity which received part of its effect perhaps from one's knowledge of his extraordinary talents. I would have taken the poet, had I had not known what he was, for a very sagacious farmer of the old Scotch school. There was a strong impression of sense and shrewdness in all his lineaments; the eye alone, I think, indicated the poetical character. It was large and dark and glowed (I say literally glowed) when he spoke with feeling and interest. I never saw such an eye in a human head, though I have seen the most distinguished men in my time.' This account is in a letter of 1827 from Scott to Lockhart, his dear son-in-law and biographer. So the letter was written more than forty years after the meeting of two of the greatest Scottish writers and a bare five years before Scott's death. Scott was well qualified to speak about distinguished men, for when he wrote this letter he had seen crowned heads of state, eminent statesmen, soldiers, sailors, clergymen, university professors, artists and other famous men. Evidently then Burns must have been a most remarkable man, and the memory of meeting him had remained fresh and vivid in Scott's mind for so long.

Below: *The town of Ayr.*

Burns on tour of Scotland, 1787

Now Burns had the opportunity to see more of his native land which he so dearly loved. This is likewise shown when in 1787 he made an agreement with James Johnson, an engraver, to help him with the latter's collection of Scottish songs. For the rest of his life Burns collected these songs and himself composed about sixty. To another publisher, Thomson, Burns gave 100 of his songs. In all there were about 250 songs. For this Burns received a few complimentary copies and £10 from Thomson. Among these songs are such gems as: 'My Love is like a red, red, Rose', 'Ye Banks and Braes o' bonnie Doon', 'A man's a man for a' that' and the immortal song of farewell, 'Auld Lang Syne'.

Chorus: *For auld lang syne, my dear,*
For auld lang syne.
We'll tak' a cup o' kindness yet,
For auld lang syne.

The Tam o' Shanter Inn at Ayr, left, commemorates Burns's poem, and the heads of Tam and his crony, Souter Johnnie, adorn the walls on either side of the front door. The picture shows him mounting his grey mare Meg.

10. Fragment — Auld lang syne —

And surely ye'll be your pint-stowp,
    And surely I'll be mine;
And we'll tak a cup o' kindness yet,
    For auld lang syne. —

We twa hae run about the braes,
    And pou't the gowans fine;
But we've wandered mony a weary fitt
    Sin auld lang syne.

We twa hae paidl't in the burn
    Frae morning sun till dine;
But seas between us braid hae roar'd
    Sin auld lang syne. —

And there's a hand
    And gie's a hand
And we'll tak a right
    For auld lang

A reproduction copy of the manuscript of **Auld Lang Syne**

The Border town of Kelso on the River Tweed. It was visited by Burns on his first tour in May 1787.

Again Burns's kindly nature comes out in the wonderful phrase – 'a cup o' kindness' – in memory of the days of old, for so we may translate 'auld lang syne'.

On his first tour, May 1787, Burns visited Duns, Kelso, Roxburgh, Jedburgh, Selkirk, Ettrick, the Braes of Yarrow and then he crossed into England, his first and last time out of Scotland. In England he made his prayer for Scotland, contained in the last two stanzas of the 'Cotter's Saturday Night', kneeling bareheaded and with uplifted hands. Next he saw Alnwick, Warkworth, Morpeth, Newcastle, Hexham and Carlisle. Later that year he visited Greenock, perhaps to see the grave of his dear 'Highland Mary', and went from there to Loch Long, Inverary, Loch Lomond, Dumbarton and Glasgow.

Then in August of this same year, 1787, Burns made a grand Highland Tour which he enjoyed very much, as millions have done and continue to do, who like Burns enjoy the lovely landscapes and lochs of the

Robert Burns by Alexander Reid. Scottish National Portrait Gallery.

Highlands in all their lambent beauty. Setting out from Edinburgh, Burns made his way to Linlithgow and then to Bannockburn, where the Scots in a memorable battle in 1314 had finally freed their land for ever from English domination. No wonder then that a patriotic Scot like Burns wrote about it so eloquently in a letter:

'The field of Bannockburn. Here no Scot can pass uninterested. I fancy to myself I see my gallant, heroic countrymen coming o'er the hill and down upon the plunderers of their country. I see my countrymen meet on the victorious field exulting in their heroic leader (King Robert the Bruce) and rescued liberty.' In a later letter Burns mentioned how he offered here 'a fervent prayer for Scotland'.

Continuing his tour, the poet went on to Stirling, Dunkeld and Blair Atholl, where he was very kindly entertained by the Duke and Duchess of Atholl. They and their 'little angel-band' of children made a great impression on him. So when he visited the famous Falls of Foyers near Loch Ness and about which he made a fine poem, he mentioned in a letter written a few days later: 'The little angel-band! I prayed for them very sincerely at the Falls of Foyers.' In a note to his poem 'The Humble Petition of Bruar Water' he wrote: 'God, Who knows all things, knows how my heart aches with gratitude whenever I recollect my reception at the noble house of Athole.' In this latter poem Burns made the Bruar Water petition the 'noble Earl of Athole' to clothe them with trees and so enhance their beauty. Such a petition worthy of Shakespeare at his best is now seen fulfilled not only at the Bruar Water but also around many other Highland streams and rivers.

During his tour Burns visited Urquhart Castle on Loch Ness where the Loch Ness monster has been seen. What a poem he could have written had he seen the monster! In Stonehaven from which district his father had come about forty years before,

Three scenes that Burns might well have enjoyed on his travels: top—Arrochar and Loch Long; middle—Inverary Castle, seat of the Dukes of Argyll; lower—Ben Lomond and Loch Lomond.

Left: *The castle at Warkworth, Northumberland, also visited by Burns in 1787.*

Stirling Castle, visited by Burns and a friend in October 1787.

he met some of his relatives. This touched him deeply. Like most Scots Burns felt very kindly towards his kith and kin. It all added up to a very memorable and enjoyable experience for the poet as the following lines show:

> *When death's dark stream I ferry o'er,*
> *(A time that surely shall come)*
> *In Heav'n itself I'll ask no more,*
> *Than just a Highland welcome.*

In October 1787 he visited Dunfermline and its noble Abbey. Here in the Abbey Church he knelt and kissed the grave of King Robert the Bruce, the great hero king of Scotland so deeply revered by Burns.

Final Years 1789–1796

In 1789 Burns, now 30, leased the farm of Ellisland on the banks of the river Nith, 6 miles from Dumfries. He also secured an appointment as an exciseman for the district. He still found time to compose great poetry, including 'Farewell to the Highlands' which Sir Walter Scott was very fond of singing, the touching lament 'To Mary in Heaven' already mentioned and that almost incomparable humorous narrative poem

The remains of Castle Urquhart on the shores of Loch Ness.

The ruins of the cathedral at Elgin.

'Tam O' Shanter'. This marvellous production of world-literature seems to have been composed in one continuous fit of inspiration. Burns was discovered by his wife in an agony of laughter reciting aloud lines of the poem he had just conceived, while the tears rolled down his cheeks. Burns considered this his best poem. Other poets have ranked it very highly indeed. Sir Walter Scott comments: 'No poet, with the exception of Shakespeare, ever possessed the power of exciting the most varied and discordant emotions with such rapid transitions.' The old Alloway Kirk (Church) and the bridge over the nearby river Doon are still to be seen and the story which Burns has embellished so marvellously has a firm basis in local legend. It is a poem which will last and be read as long as English or rather Scots lasts and is read!

The poet was now happily married to Jean Armour. Of her he once said: 'She has the sweetest temper and the kindest heart in the country.' And what an understanding wife she was. She nursed a natural child of her husband along with one common to them both. When asked if she had twins, she smiled and replied: 'No. The other bairn (child) belongs to a neighbour and I am taking care of it.' This is surely one of the most discreet, kind and self-sacrificing actions any wife could ever accomplish.

With all his literary work and other duties Burns found it difficult to give his farm at Ellisland the attention it required. So in 1791 he gave up the lease and made his home in Dumfries. His work for the customs and excise entailed much riding around his district. He performed his duties well and knew when to be lenient when no principle was at stake. At a country fair he said to a poor widow selling unlicensed ale: 'Kate,

Top: *The awesome ramparts of Castle Campbell.*

Left: *Dunfermline Abbey where Burns knelt to kiss the gravestone of Robert the Bruce.*

Right: *A copy of the bust of Burns by Sir John Steele, R.S.A., executed for Poet's Corner in Westminster Abbey.*

are you mad? Do you no' ken (not know) that the supervisor and I will be upon you in 40 minutes? Guid-bye the noo.' (Good-bye just now.) The kindly hint was taken. Kate was not to be seen when Burns arrived with his supervisor. Burns's work was praised by his superiors. One of them remarked at a meeting of the Excise Court: 'Let me look at the books of Burns. They show that an upright officer may also be a merciful one.' In this same year, 1791, the poet bravely boarded and seized a smugglers' ship in the Solway Firth near Dumfries.

By 1794 Burns's family consisted of four boys and one girl. Another boy was born a few days after the poet's death in 1796. In addition to being a kind husband Burns was also a tender and loving father. J. Gray, who taught Burns's children, and who knew Burns well, made this comment on their father: 'He was a kind and attentive father and took great delight in spending his evenings cultivating his children's minds. Their education was the grand object of his life. He took great pains to train them to think and to reflect and to keep them pure from every form of vice. This he considered a sacred duty which he kept up till his last illness.'

During these last five years of his life, 1791–6, Burns produced some of his best poems and songs. Among them are 'Lament of Mary, Queen of Scots', which Burns was very glad to have written and which also reflects his sincere patriotism, 'Scots wha'

The home of the Burns family at Mauchline, Ayrshire (now the Strathclyde Region), where he set up house with his wife, Jean Armour.

hae' – the song of King Robert the Bruce
and his soldiers before the battle of
Bannockburn (1314), 'The Rights of
Women' – which shows Burns as a true
gentleman – 'An Ode to Liberty', 'Charlie,
he's my Darling' – in praise of Bonnie Prince
Charlie, the leader of the famous 1745
Jacobite Rising, 'Contented wi' little and
cantie (happy) wi' mair (more)' – surely a
very human song, 'My wife's a winsome
wee thing' and finally his immortal song
'A man's a man for a' that'. This song
endeared him to Queen Victoria (1837–
1901), who was better pleased with this than
with anything else he had written.

Burns's House, Dumfries, where the poet died in 1796.

Below: *The River Nith at Dumfries.*

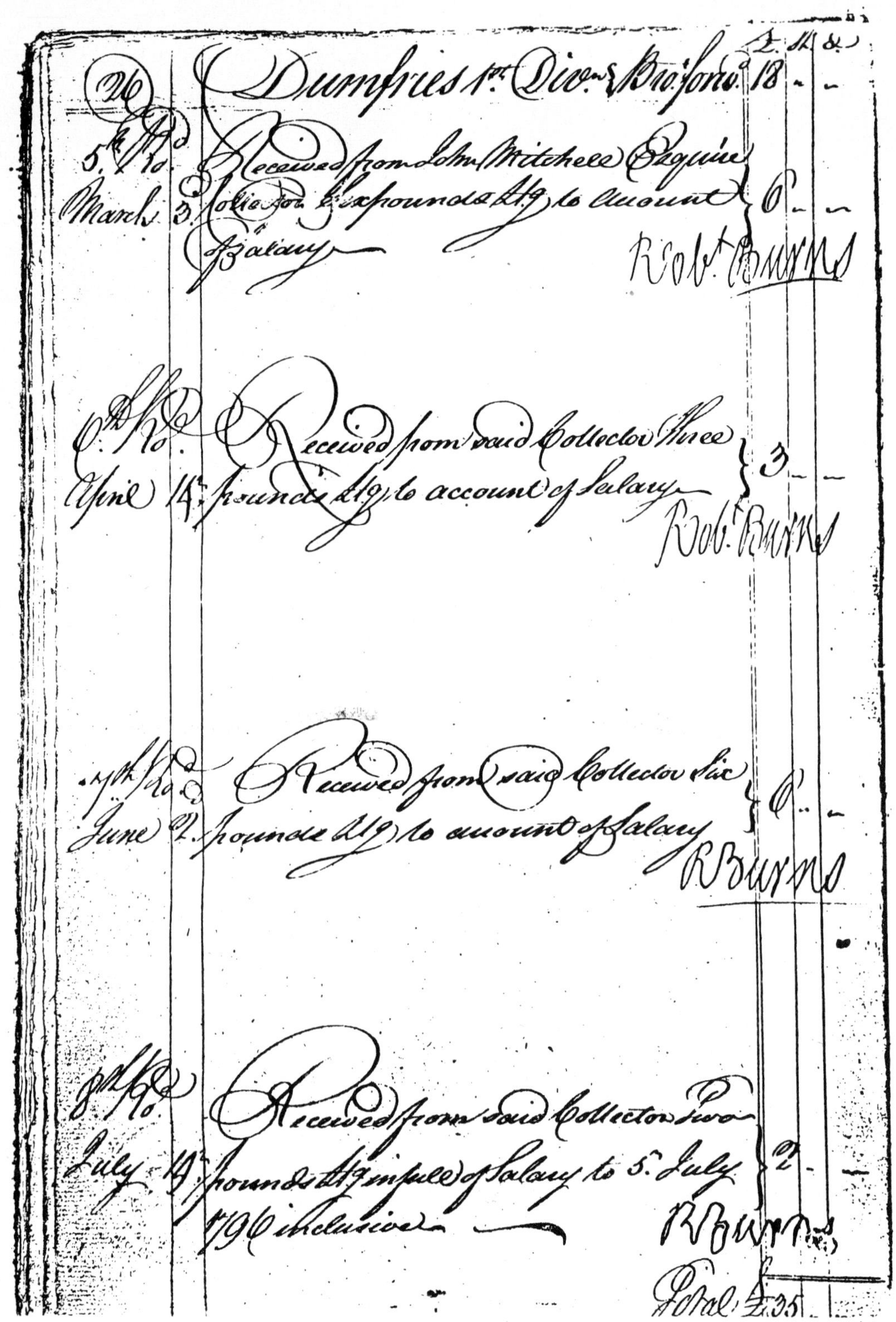

A document signed by Burns in the last month of his life. Note how shakily he has written his signature.

Burns is loved by millions of ordinary folk all over the world, among them being the Russians who have a very fine translation from the great Soviet poet, S. Marshak. In 1959 an anthology of his poems was translated into Chinese. One feels that the Russian and Chinese peoples, like the Scots, will find much enjoyment from the writings of a poet with a background so similar to millions of their own good people. And all this from a man with little formal education who died before he was 38 years old.

Now the end was near. Burns had worked hard all his life both in his farming and official duties. He had loyally supported his wife and children, though he rarely had much money, and indeed at times he was very poorly off. He made very little from his writing and almost nothing as we have seen from the wonderful collection of Scottish songs for which he was chiefly responsible. To write Scottish songs to be set to Scottish tunes was the greatest delight for Burns, as he felt that in this way his fame would be immortal. It was immortal in other ways as well.

By 1796 his health had greatly deteriorated. He went for treatment to the coast of the Solway Firth near Dumfries. It was too late. On 18th July, 1796, he returned home. He knew he was dying. To his wife he prophesied: 'Ay, Jean. They'll think much more of me a hundred years after this.' Then his sense of humour came back. Thinking of the Volunteer Corps formed to repel a possible French invasion and of which he was a member, he said: 'Don't let the awkward squad fire over my grave.' This was in allusion to the three volleys fired over the grave of one of their members. On 21st July, 1796, the great poet gently breathed his last. On 25th July he was buried in St Michael's Churchyard, Dumfries, with full military honours in the presence of a vast crowd from far and near. Three straggling volleys were fired over his humble grave. Burns would have smiled.

The Auld Brig o' Doon at Alloway, immortalized in the famous song.

The mausoleum, St Michael's churchyard, Dumfries

Burns Today

Scots in their country's heroic history hold four men high in honour – Wallace and Bruce, Scott and Burns. Wallace and Bruce forged the independent nation. Scott and Burns gave that nation an assured place in world-literature. Wallace and Bruce represent the Catholic strand, Scott the Episcopalian and Burns the Presbyterian strand, three strands which have all contributed much to the weft and web of Scotland's glory. In these ecumenical days may the weft and web of these three valuable strands produce the seamless robe of union of the Christian Churches of Scotland, which Wallace and Bruce, Scott and Burns, if alive today, would, as kindly Scots, promote with united mind and heart and with all their varied gifts and talents which have meant so much in our epic Scottish story.

So now we take our leave of this great poet, this man for all men and for all seasons, humbly grateful to have been solaced by his wit and wisdom, by his lyric beauty of song and poetry and by his immortal memory. Humbly he himself would add:

A MAN'S A MAN FOR A' THAT.

A HUMBLE TRIBUTE TO ROBERT BURNS FROM A FELLOW SCOT

For a' the Scots the chiel[1] they love,
His honest worth ennobles our race.
For chiels elsewhere a man above
The ups and downs of honours and place.

He speaks to Scots; he speaks to a',
A man's a man for a' that.
A man he was in spite of a',
Sincere and kind – so is the chap.

His faults he tells and does not hide.
He fell, he rose – so can we all.
Aye may his spirit wi' us bide –
Greatness gained from failings fought.

Man of vision and contemplation,
Man of glorious exultation,
Man of heart and much compassion,
Mice and men in you find fusion.

Man of human understanding,
Man of gentle forgiving,
Man of duty, yet overlooking,
Peccadilloes nae[2] worth noticing.

Dogs and hare and mouse and mare
You make us love and for them care,
All things of worth we too can share
And love as you did mair[3] an' mair.

J. A. CARRUTH
31–12–70

[1] person.　　[2] not.　　[3] more.

Chief works of Robert Burns (1759–1796)

1773	Aged 14	*Song*	*Handsome Nell.*
1775	Aged 16	*Song*	*O Tibbie, I hae seen the day.*
1778	Aged 19	*Poem*	*The Tarbolton Lasses.*
1781	Aged 22	*Poem*	*A Prayer in the Prospect of Death* (paraphrase of Psalm I).
1783	Aged 24	*Song*	*Green grow the Rashes.*
1784	Aged 25	*Poems*	*Epitaph on my ever honoured Father. Man was made to mourn: A Dirge.*
1785	Aged 26	*Poem*	*Holy Willie's Prayer.*
		Song	*Rantin', Rovin' Robin.*
		Poems	*Halloween. To a Mouse. The Cotter's Saturday Night.*
		Poems	*Address to the Deil. Scotch Drink. The Twa Dogs.*

1786	Aged 27	*Poems*	*Address to the Unco Guid. To u Louse. The Holy Fair.*
		Poems	*To a Mountain Daisy. My Highland Lassie, O. The Brigs of Ayr.*
		Poems	*Lines written on a Bank Note. Stanzas on Naething.*
		Poems	*Address to Edinburgh. Address to a Haggis.*
1787	Aged 28	*Poems*	*Elegy on the death of Sir James Hunter Blair. Lines on the Fall of Foyers.*
		Poem	*Birthday Ode* for Prince Charles Edward Stuart.
		Poems	*Clarinda* – Mrs A. M'Lehose.
1788	Aged 29	*Poem*	*The Chevalier's Lament* (supposedly sung by Prince Charles after Culloden).
		Poem	*O were I on Parnassus Hill* in praise of his wife, 'bonnie Jean'.
		Song	*Auld Lang Syne.* A world-famous song.
1789	Aged 30	*Poems*	*The wounded hare. John Anderson, my Jo.*
		Songs	*Ca' the Yowes to the Knowes. Farewell to the Highlands.*
		Poems	*To Mary in Heaven.* In praise of Highland Mary. *Address to the Toothache.*
1790	Aged 31	*Poem*	*The Gowden Locks of Anna.*
		Poem	*Tam O' Shanter.* Considered by Burns to be his best work.
1791	Aged 32	*Poems*	*On the Birth of a posthumous Child. Lament on Mary, Queen of Scots.*
		Songs	*The Banks O' Doon – Ye banks and braes O' bonnie Doon. Sweet Afton.*
		Poem	*A Grace before Dinner, Extempore. A Grace after Dinner, Extempore.*
		Song	*Parting Song to Clarinda.*
1792	Aged 33	*Songs*	*The Deil's Awa' Wi' Th' Exciseman. My Wife's a winsome wee Thing.*
		Song	*Highland Mary.*
		Poem	*The Rights of Woman.*
		Song	*Duncan Gray cam' here to woo.*
1793	Aged 34	*Song*	*Bruce's March to Bannockburn – Scots wha' hae.*
1794	Aged 35	*Songs*	*A red, red Rose. My Love is like a red, red rose. The Lovely Lass O' Inverness.*
		Songs	*Charlie, he's my darling. It was a' for our rightfu' King.*
		Poem	*An Ode to Liberty.*
		Song	*Contented wi' little and cantie* (happy) *wi' mair* (more).
1795	Aged 36	*Songs*	*A Man's a Man for a' that. Does haughty Gaul invasion threat?*
1796	Aged 37	*Song*	*Fairest Maid on Devon Banks*, written 9 days before he died.

In addition Burns wrote the following:

1783–1785 *First Common-Place Book.* (Notes, Song, Scraps by Robt. Burness.)

1786 *Second Common-Place Book.* Contains 15 of the poet's works all in his own writing and his notes on them.

Autobiography from his birth till 1787 when he was aged 28.

543 letters from 1780, aged 23, to 18th July, 1796, three days before his death.

Edinburgh Journal, 1787.

Chronology of Life and Works of Robert Burns

1759 January 25 Robert Burns born at Alloway, near Ayr. His father, William Burness or Burnes, was from Kincardineshire. His mother, formerly Agnes Brown, was from Carrick, Ayrshire. (In 1786 Robert modified his family name to 'Burns', the usual form of the name in Ayrshire.)

1765 6 years old Robert at school at Alloway. His excellent teacher, John Murdoch, gave him a good grounding in English language and literature. At home Burns spoke Lowland Scots in which he wrote some of his best poems and songs.

1769 10 years old Murdoch left. Betty Davidson, an old woman staying with the family, helped the poetical talent germinating in Robert by her many tales, songs, ghost-stories and historical and legendary lore.

1770 11 years old Burns's father taught Robert arithmetic, geography, natural history, Christian doctrine and English literature.